Original title:
Foliage Follies

Copyright © 2025 Creative Arts Management OÜ
All rights reserved.

Author: Alec Davenport
ISBN HARDBACK: 978-1-80567-390-3
ISBN PAPERBACK: 978-1-80567-689-8

The Dance of Decay and Birth

Leaves twirl and twist in the breeze,
Whispering secrets, full of tease.
Once bright and bold, now wrinkled and bare,
They dance like clowns without a care.

Roots tangle up in a game of tag,
While mushrooms pop up, a colorful brag.
Nature's theater with all its plots,
Where laughter echoes and humor's caught.

Clusters of Chaos Amongst the Calm

In a patch of green, a ruckus ensues,
Squirrels organizing their acorn views.
Each nut misplaced, they scratch their heads,
A comedy troupe playing tricks instead.

A rabbit hops through, chasing a leaf,
While snails giggle slow, with no hint of grief.
The patchwork of chaos, a sight to behold,
As ants carry crumbs like stories retold.

The Unruly Edge of the Forest

At the forest's edge, it's quite a sight,
Branches bicker, what a hilarious fight!
The bushes gossip, in murmurs and sighs,
While vines intertwine, plotting their lies.

A chipmunk flips over, in playful surprise,
Beneath the tall grass, where the silliness lies.
The trees stand tall, but with laughter, they sway,
In nature's grand circus, come join the fray!

Vibrant Hues and Hidden Views

Colors collide in a whimsical show,
Tulips winking, putting on their glow.
Daisies chuckle, while poppies parade,
A floral fiesta, where no one's afraid.

Beneath the bright canopies, secrets are spun,
Whimsical whispers, oh, what fun!
The petals giggle, at tricks of the sun,
In a world where humor and beauty run.

Echoes of the Emerald Enigma

A squirrel in a hat, oh what a sight,
Chasing shadows from morning till night.
A dance of the leaves, a rustling tease,
They laugh in the breeze with comical ease.

With twigs for a cane and acorns in tow,
Sipping dew drops, putting on quite the show.
The trees start to giggle as branches sway,
In a jestful parade where the whimsy holds sway.

Fractured Mosaics of Greenery

In a patchwork of colors, the garden plays,
Fluffy clouds toss in spontaneous ways.
The daisies gossip with the tulips so grand,
While the daffodils chuckle, just can't understand.

A bumblebee waltzes, unaware of the dance,
As the ferns share secrets in leafy romance.
Petals tumble and giggle, spin round and around,
In a jolly confusion, their mirth knows no bounds.

Arboreal Antics and Adventures

An owl wearing glasses reads stories of lore,
While the rabbits debate if they're ever quite sure.
The hedgehogs host parties with snacks from the trees,
As the sun peeks in to join in with the tease.

Frogs make a splash, they jump with delight,
Launching past lilies, oh, what a sight!
The branches are laughing, there's mischief in air,
In this lively realm, there's joy everywhere.

The Spiral of the Wisteria Whirl

Round and around in a viney embrace,
Giggling petals, a whimsical race.
Fragrant confetti floats soft in the sun,
As hummingbirds dart, in a buzz they have fun.

Twisting and turning like ribbons of cheer,
The blossoms conspire, a trickster's frontier.
With tendrils that tickle and colors that play,
Nature's own carnival brightens the day.

Wildflowers' Whimsical Whispers

In a meadow, blooms do prance,
They sway around like they can dance.
A daisy giggles, quite a tease,
While buttercups play games with bees.

Tulips chat with a cheerful tone,
While sunflowers boast of being grown.
A clover tells a silly joke,
As dandelions start to poke.

The wind joins in with a playful shove,
As petals flutter, all in love.
With every rustle, laughter flows,
In fields where nature's humor glows.

So let us join this flowery spree,
Where blooms concoct their jubilee.
With every stem, a tale unfolds,
In whispers soft, each story told.

The Turbulent Tides of Botanic Bliss

In garden beds where veggies dream,
The carrots plot, it seems a scheme.
Potatoes wiggle, full of surprise,
While beets attempt to don disguise.

Flowers frown at their leafy kin,
As radishes boast of the color skin.
Cucumbers giggle, not so shy,
With tendrils trying to reach the sky.

The herbs concoct a zany plan,
To tickle the toes of a passing man.
Thyme and basil, a fragrant tease,
Sway in laughter with the gentle breeze.

As fruits dangle from their leafy thrones,
Bananas fall, creating groans.
Each sprout is part of this clever game,
In a botanic world, wild and untame.

Exuberance in Every Leafy Corner

In the garden's laughter, plants do dance,
Bouncing around in their green romance.
Petals tickle bees, like a silly prank,
Wiggly worms smile, well, don't they just tank?

Sunlight sprinkles joy, a cheerful glow,
Grass tickles toes, in a playful show.
A daffodil stumbles, oh what a sight,
As daisies gossip under skies so bright.

The Soft Embrace of the Undergrowth

Sneaky ferns curl up, like a cozy cat,
Hiding from the squirrel, like, 'Where's he at?'
Mushrooms pop up, wearing polka dot hats,
While crickets serenade with silly chats.

Thorns play peek-a-boo, in bushes they dwell,
While a rose rolls its eyes, not voting so well.
A prickly affair, yet laughter will flow,
In the soft embrace where shadows grow.

Radiant Ruins of the Shaded Realm

Once regal leaves turn to carpets of fun,
Beneath old oaks where the sunlight can't run.
A lost acorn chuckles, thinking it's ripe,
While branches above do a comic-type swipe.

Beneath shady canopies, whispers abound,
As squirrels drop nuts which softly rebound.
The trees hold their breath, just waiting to see,
Which critter will slip, oh dear, not me!

Whirling in the Autumnal Air

Breezes come dancing, leaves swirl about,
Crisp crunching giggles, a fluttering shout.
A maple leaf twirls like it's lost in a ball,
While others just tumble, and yell, 'Oh, fall!'

Pumpkins roll over, cracking each grin,
As squirrels look puzzled, 'Where do we begin?'
Colors parade in a riotous spree,
In the cheerful chaos, there's joy, can't you see?

The Lament of Lost Petals

Petals flutter down like failed dreams,
They giggle as they're caught in streams.
A flower's wish, so sweet and grand,
Yet here they float, with no command.

Once vibrant hues now fade away,
They blush in shame, as if to say,
"Who knew the ground could be so tough?"
While teasing winds just call their bluff.

Tangles of the Tranquil Thicket

In thickets thick, where branches weave,
A squirrel schemes, you won't believe.
He trips on vines, a comic splash,
While laughing leaves join in the crash.

With every twist, a creaky groan,
The forest plays with critters' tone.
A mess of roots, a jester's nest,
It's nature's stage, a true forest fest.

Secrets Beneath the Canopy

Beneath the leaves, where shadows play,
A world of whispers wades away.
A snail debates his slow parade,
While beetles plot their grand charade.

Secrets murmur in the breeze,
A chipmunk's joke brings all to knees.
"Three acorns walk into a bar!"
He cackles loud, they roll afar.

Rustling Stories of Autumn's Breath

As autumn breathes through amber trees,
Gusts tickle leaves, they laugh with ease.
Each crinkled twist tells tales of cheer,
  Of playful pranks from yesteryear.

With every gust, the tales unfold,
Of acorn thieves and bravado bold.
A cascade of colors, a lively spree,
  Nature's jesters, all wild and free.

Whispers of Autumn's Grace

Leaves giggle as they fall,
Swirling like a waltz in the hall.
Squirrels plotting in their haste,
Chasing acorns, what a taste!

Jack Frost sneaks with chilly glee,
Wearing mittens, can't you see?
Pumpkins chuckling in the patch,
Whisper secrets, no need to hatch.

Crisp air dances with delight,
Spinning stories, day and night.
A tapestry of colors bright,
Nature's humor, pure and light.

Dance of the Leafy Shadows

Trees shuffle to a breezy tune,
Leaves all twirling, very soon.
A squirrel dances with a grin,
As shadows cast their leafy spin.

Branches creak with laughter loud,
As crows gather, a cheeky crowd.
Laughter echoes, soft and sweet,
While critters prance on nimble feet.

Dappled sunbeams join the spree,
Nature's jest, so wild and free.
A playful game hides in the shade,
Where friendships bloom and joy is made.

Laughter Beneath the Canopy

Underneath the leafy roof,
Bugs hum jokes, oh what a goof!
A chipmunk wears a tiny hat,
Winking at a chatty brat.

The sun ticks off the day with cheer,
As squirrels race, then disappear.
Mushrooms peek with such surprise,
Trying hard to hide their eyes.

The branches sway, a giggling crew,
Tickled by the gentle dew.
Nature's jests all around,
Making laughter quite profound.

Secrets of the Verdant Realm

In jungles thick with leafy dreams,
Lizards whisper playful schemes.
A dandelion blows with zest,
Sending seeds on a daring quest.

Treetops giggle in the breeze,
As shadows play, a cheeky tease.
Flowers bow and sway their heads,
As snails shuffle off to bed.

The forest holds its secrets tight,
Jokes exchanged beneath the light.
A symphony of giggles roam,
In verdant lands, we feel at home.

Antics of the Swaying Sprigs

In the breeze they sway and spin,
Dancing leaves with a cheeky grin.
Twisting to the left, then the right,
Making every passerby delight.

A leaf tickles a passing nose,
While another plays peekaboo with crows.
Laughter rustles through the trees,
Nature's giggle carried on the breeze.

Medley of Mischief Underneath

Beneath the boughs, a riot of cheer,
Where acorns plot, oh dear, oh dear!
Squirrels giggle in nutty delight,
As shadows dance in the fading light.

A plump mushroom wears a hat,
As a startled beetle goes splat!
Jigs and jives with each little quirk,
In the thicket where mischief lurks.

The Folly of Nature's Palette

Colors clash in a vibrant spree,
A pink fern sings to a green pea.
The daisies debate who's the fairest one,
While daisies and daffodils frolic in fun.

A butterfly whispers, 'Look at me!'
As a dandelion goes 'Puff!' with glee.
Nature's colors in playful strife,
Creating a canvas of whimsical life.

Whimsy Within the Green Cloak

Under the cloak of emerald hue,
A raccoon insists on wearing a shoe.
With flowers as crowns and vines for ties,
The forest dances beneath sunny skies.

A rabbit juggles acorns with flair,
While a wise old owl just stops to stare.
Amongst the giggles, the gusts do play,
Crafting a symphony of a leafy ballet.

Playful Patterns in the Understory

In the shade where shadows play,
Leaves dance like children, come what may.
Twisting, turning, without a care,
Nature's laughter fills the air.

Here a squirrel does a silly jig,
Twirling round like a vibrant twig.
Grasshoppers join in with a leap,
While butterflies prance, their colors deep.

The bushes giggle, swaying low,
As gentle winds create a show.
Oh, what fun beneath the trees,
A festival of whispers and breezy teas.

Every leaf a story told,
In hues of green and hints of gold.
Together they form a merry ring,
In this playground where nature sings.

Enchantment in the Emerald Maze

Inside the maze of leafy cheer,
A raccoon stumbles, full of beer.
He tips his hat, gives a sly wink,
And tumbles over with a clink!

Mossy paths that twist and wind,
Lead us where the friendly beehive's blind.
Giggling bees in a flurry dance,
Whispering secrets in a buzzing trance.

The greenery chuckles at every turn,
As ferns mimic a flamenco's burn.
With every step, the mischief grows,
In this maze where each plant glows.

So tiptoe lightly, do not stray,
For laughter thrives in this leafy ballet.
In the emerald tangle, joy is found,
Where silliness and plant life abound.

When the Trees Tell Tales

Listen close to the tree's delight,
Telling tales in the gentle night.
With a creak and a groan, they spin their yarn,
Of brave little creatures wearing no charm.

The oak grins wide, its bark like skin,
Recalling the days when the squirrel wore thin.
A chipmunk's quest for a shiny prize,
Leaves everyone giggling, oh how time flies!

The willow bends, whispering sweet,
Of love-struck bunnies that met by the creek.
They snicker at moose who thought they could dance,
But tripped on their hooves in a wild romance.

In the rustling leaves, where secrets soar,
Tall tales of nature are never a bore.
So lean in closely, hear the cheery chime,
These wise old trees have humor in rhyme.

The Jive of the Fluttering Foliage

Leaves shake and shimmy, take the floor,
Clapping hands of acorns, calling for more.
Twigs tap out a rhythmic beat,
While crickets chirp, oh what a treat!

A butterfly wears shoes of gold,
As he struts by, both bold and cold.
With every flutter, he brings the funk,
The forest boogies, no time to junk.

Dancing dandelions wave their heads,
Join in the whirl 'til the sun bled.
Even the shadows step in line,
For a raucous party, oh so divine.

So sway with the breeze, let your heart rise,
In the ballet of branches beneath the skies.
The jive goes on till the stars appear,
Nature's celebratory, silly cheer!

Lush Hijinks Beneath the Boughs

Leaves dance lightly in the breeze,
Branches jiggle with playful ease.
Acorns drop like little bombs,
Squirrels laugh in nature's psalms.

Underneath the leafy spread,
Chasing shadows, where dreams tread.
A picnic set, oh what a sight,
Someone's sandwich flies in flight!

Beneath the boughs, a giggle stirs,
Nature's jesters, a thousand furs.
Twirling vines, they tease and play,
Who knew trees would join the fray?

Watch the flowers do a dance,
Petals wobble, take a chance.
In this riot of color and cheer,
Laughter blossoms, crystal clear.

The Kaleidoscope of Nature's Whimsy

Colors clash, a riot bright,
Butterflies dance in pure delight.
Tulips giggle, daisies beam,
Nature's canvas, a wild dream.

A caterpillar slips and slides,
Through leafy greens, where fun resides.
It wriggles 'round, a joyful sight,
A busy artist in daylight.

Clouds wear capes, a floating show,
Rainbows arch with a merry glow.
Puddles splash, a chorus sings,
Nature's charm pulls all the strings.

Laughter echoed in the trees,
Whispers float upon the breeze.
In this world, the silly reigns,
Joyful chaos, like wild trains.

Autumn's Prankster Parade

Crisp leaves crunch beneath each tread,
While pumpkins smile, eyes full of dread.
The wind snickers, a playful tease,
As taffy sticks upon the trees.

Mischief lurks in every hue,
Squirrels plan their heist anew.
A sudden gust sends hats afloat,
And laughter rides on each small boat.

Spooky shadows peek and blend,
With giggling ghosts that twist and bend.
Candy corn rolls off the plate,
Nature's sweets that tease our fate.

Leaves wear sweaters, snug and neat,
As critters dance on tiny feet.
In this parade of jokester flair,
Autumn's laughter fills the air.

Revelations in the Thicket's Laughter

In the thicket, glee awakes,
The bushes chuckle, just for grakes.
A rabbit hops, it's all a game,
While hidden critters join the fame.

A flower sneezes with a flare,
As bees buzz 'round without a care.
Giggles spill from every leaf,
Nature's jesters, beyond belief.

Shrubs embrace, in cheeky cheer,
Whispers dizzy in the atmosphere.
Moments caught, like flashes bright,
In every corner, pure delight.

Cackling frogs start quite a show,
With their croaks, laughter flows.
In this thicket of green surprise,
Joy erupts before our eyes.

The Fractured Palette of Nature

Colors clash in each green leaf,
Screaming hues without belief.
A purple bush next to a lime,
Nature's joke, a funny rhyme.

The flowers dance in mismatched shoes,
With petals painted in absurd views.
A rainbow sprout on Tuesday's glee,
A thorny grin, just wait and see!

Shadows stretch and giggle loud,
As bees wear stripes, but feel so proud.
Glimpses of whimsy twist and sway,
In this palette, night steals the day.

Tangles and Twists of Verdant Life

Vines entwined like lovers' arms,
Whispering secrets, sharing charms.
A lopsided tree with roots that prance,
Rewards the squirrel a nutty chance.

Butterflies wear polka dot suits,
While crickets play their funny flutes.
Tangled branches laugh and jest,
In this wild home, they're all at rest.

A snail in slippers on the trail,
Moves slow, but dreams up grand tales.
With every twist, a silly grin,
In this world, fun's always in!

An Ode to Overgrown Dreams

In the garden of wild schemes,
Everything grows beyond its dreams.
A pumpkin dances, clumsy and round,
Where tangled wishes are unbound.

A sunflower bows, a hat askew,
While daisies boast a funky view.
The carrots plot a secret run,
As beetles laugh and catch the fun.

Each petal shouts, a zany tune,
With shadows prancing 'neath the moon.
Overgrown hopes, sprouting laughter bright,
In dreams that tickle through the night!

Melodies of the Muddled Meadow

In the meadow, where jam is thick,
The daisies giggle, their stems all stick.
A goat strums grass like a violin,
Producing tunes of a funny grin.

Buttercups wear hats made of dew,
While odd creatures dance to a tune askew.
The butterflies flutter, twirl and spin,
In this muddled place, where laughs begin.

A frog croaks out a saxophone beat,
Joined by crickets tapping their feet.
Amidst the chaos, joy does flow,
In this meadow, laughter's the show!

The Jester of Greenery

In the meadow where shadows play,
A jester dances, bright and gay.
His leafy hat, a sight to see,
Tickles the grass, wild with glee.

With every tumble, he makes a joke,
Leaves giggle softly, all awoke.
Beneath the oak, his antics rise,
As twigs bow down and branches sigh.

He juggles acorns, one and two,
A squirrel laughs, joins in the brew.
With every twist and flip so grand,
The flowers chuckle, hand in hand.

At sunset's call, the forest roars,
As laughter echoes, nature soars.
The jester prances, day is done,
In this folly, all is fun!

Tumble of the Golden Leaves

Golden leaves in a swirling dance,
Tumble down with a playful chance.
They skip and roll on the breezy ground,
Making music, a rustling sound.

Squirrels chase in a frenzied race,
Gathering treasures, trying to chase.
Each leap they take, a laugh they send,
In the tumble, around each bend.

The wind joins in, with a whoosh and a sway,
"Catch me if you can!" it seems to say.
Leaves giggle softly, spinning around,
Tickled by the joy that's all around.

At twilight's curtain, they settle down,
Cradled by night, wear a golden gown.
In this fun spree, life takes a spin,
With a chuckling heart, let the joy begin!

Serenade of the Shimmering Sprouts

Little sprouts sing a bubbly tune,
Beneath the sun and a merry moon.
They wiggle and sway in the gentle breeze,
With whispered secrets, they aim to please.

Each sprout a story just waiting to share,
Of beetles and bugs, of hops and air.
They chuckle and snicker, so full of cheer,
In this tiny concert, all can hear.

A raindrop joins with a plink and a pop,
Creating a rhythm, they can't stop.
The daisies laugh, joining the show,
As laughter blossoms, rooted below.

With every flicker and glimmer of light,
The sprouts throw a dance, a vibrant sight.
In this serenade of glee and sprout,
Every giggle and smile, never a doubt!

Mischief Among the Branches

Up high where the branches bend and sway,
    Mischief brews in a playful way.
  A raccoon giggles, a crow lets out caw,
   As pranks unfold with a humorous awe.

     A squirrel leaps, a daring feat,
   Stirring up laughter, oh what a treat!
With a flick of his tail, he teases the breeze,
   As laughter rings out among the trees.

The leaves whisper jokes, rustling with glee,
     As branches sway, in harmony.
   Buds holding giggles, secrets to keep,
   In this woodland, where spirits leap.

  As twilight falls, mischief won't stop,
  With giggling stars, they pop and hop.
   Among the branches, joy takes flight,
 In this merry place, deep into the night!

The Spirited Soiree of the Shrubs

In the garden where greens declare,
Shrubs dance wildly, without a care.
They twist and twirl in bright array,
Singing tunes that keep gloom at bay.

Petals laugh, they shimmy and shake,
In the breezy gust, they jive and break.
With worms as guests and ants in a line,
They sip on dew, feeling divine.

A party that no one can resist,
With each little bloom adding a twist.
The sun jests down with a playful wink,
While butterflies join, fluttering in sync.

And as twilight drapes its gentle veil,
The shrubs giggle and share a tale.
Of radishes dressed up as stars,
In this festivity beneath the jars.

Bushes Full of Boldness

Bold bushes boast with leafy pride,
Their branches sway, like arms open wide.
Each shrub declares, with voice so grand,
'Come share my shade, let's make a stand!'

They gossip secrets of leaves so lush,
Whispering tales in the evening hush.
With flowers chatty amidst the green,
A raucous gathering, a lively scene.

Squirrels scamper, a jesting crew,
They'll juggle acorns, a leafy zoo.
Rabbits tap dance, their whiskers a-flare,
In this thrilling bush, everyone's there.

But watch your step, for here's a clue:
A thistle's prickle might play a joke too.
With laughter and cheer, the bushes stand tall,
In their leafy kingdom, there's fun for all.

A Telling of Hidden Pathways

Wandering trails, with secrets abound,
Nestled in leaves, where giggles resound.
Every pathway winks with delight,
Inviting the brave hearts to take flight.

Twisting and turning, adventures await,
Where hedges frolic and rabbits debate.
Each corner holds stories so grand,
With daisies plotting, their mischief well planned.

A thicket of whispers and rustles of glee,
Follow the sounds, join the jubilee!
With every step, anticipation grows,
Among contrary thorns where hilarity flows.

And as the moon spills silver on ground,
The pathways chuckle, laughter profound.
In this woodland play, so wildly free,
Each twist and turn, a riddle to see.

Crinkled Pages of the Earth

Crinkled pages of earth's own book,
Where creatures gather and laughter is took.
Leaves turn stories, tales bound in curls,
In the humor of nature, magic unfurls.

With ants as narrators of everyday quests,
And snails with tales they think are the best.
Each pore and wrinkle holds words so bright,
From dew-kissed mornings to warm starry nights.

The wind whispers secrets, weaving through trees,
While blossoms share gossip on a playful breeze.
Petal to petal, the laughter spreads round,
In this library of life, joys abound.

So read the pages, both vivid and worn,
Hear the jesters in gardens, so richly adorned.
With every rustle and crinkle that's heard,
The tales celebrate life, nature's own word.

The Journey of the Curling Leaf

A leaf pirouettes on a gusty breeze,
Spinning 'round like a dancer with ease.
It twirls by a squirrel, who stares in surprise,
As it dips and it dives, oh, what a disguise!

Down to the ground, what a bumpy descent,
It lands on a frog, who was quite content.
With a bounce and a leap, they both start to grin,
Together they roll, let the leaf party begin!

They glide through the grass, over flowers they roam,
Creating a ruckus, when no one's at home.
A slip on a puddle, oh what a sight,
The frog quacks like a duck, in laughter and light!

So off goes the leaf, on its whimsical quest,
A journey of joy, never wanting to rest.
With giggles and wiggles, they dance 'neath the sun,
For a leaf and a frog, it's all just good fun!

Ferocious Foliage in the Wind

The trees start to shiver, their leaves in a fight,
Twirling and swirling in dizzy delight.
A battle begins, but what's the big fuss?
It's just a strong breeze, causing all of this!

A cactus nearby, so prickly and proud,
Watches the chaos with leaves in a crowd.
"Watch out for me!" yells a bold little sprout,
"I'll show you real fury, just watch me shout!"

The petals are flapping, they huddle and cower,
As gusts spin them round like a flowing shower.
The world is a carnival, wild with a rush,
Leaves laugh and they cheer, in a colorful hush!

When calmness returns, they settle in place,
Exhausted but joyful, not losing their grace.
Those fierce little dancers, they'll bicker and roam,
Yet every wild storm just feels like a home!

Paintbrush of the Earth

A brush dipped in colors, the Earth starts to sway,
With strokes full of giggles, it brightens the day.
Blotches of laughter, each tree wears a grin,
As flowers burst open, let the joy spill in!

Yellow and orange in a playful splash,
The wind carries whispers, a colorful dash.
Rivers of purple run down from the hills,
As butterflies flutter, embracing the thrills.

With every new stroke, more chuckles unfold,
Creating a canvas that never gets old.
From green to magenta, it dances and beams,
A paintbrush so merry, it colors our dreams!

So join in the laughter, get lost in the hues,
For nature's a party, just waiting for you.
Let's paint all together, with tickles and cheer,
A world so vibrant, bringing fun ever near!

Kaleidoscope of Kinetic Colors

A jumble of hues in a whirl and a spin,
Leaves leap and they laugh, as the wind pulls them in.
Dancing like children, from twig to the ground,
In this merry chaos, pure joy can be found.

A rainbow of shapes, from striped to the spot,
They jiggle and wiggle, as if caught in a pot.
With splashes of crimson, bright teal, and lime,
This riot of color dances through time.

As acorns tumble down, they join in the fray,
Rolling with glee, they shout hip-hip-hooray!
In a tapestry vibrant, they weave through the air,
Creating a spectacle, with style and flair!

So come join the circus of colors at play,
With laughter and giggles to brighten your day.
A kaleidoscope world, spinning bursts of delight,
With leaves as the stars, it's a beautiful sight!

Unkempt Gardens of the Heart

In a junkyard of blooms, oh what a sight,
Weeds wear crowns, feeling quite bright.
A gnome lost his hat, now he's a thief,
Pursuing the prize, causing much grief.

Sunflowers gossip, hats tipped to the side,
Rabbits in bowties take a long glide.
Petunias giggle, dancing with glee,
A butterfly squeals, "Look at me!"

Daisies wear glasses, pretending to read,
While roses in pajamas munch on some seed.
Tangled in laughter, the garden's a mess,
Yet in its chaos, no one would guess!

So here's to the heart, a wild old place,
Where love can grow wild, yet full of grace.
A tangle of joy in every sweet chart,
Celebrating the unkempt gardens of heart.

Swaying Silhouettes at Dusk

Under the twilight, shadows come alive,
Trees twist and twirl, in a jolly jive.
A squirrel's on point, with moves so slick,
Tripping on acorns, oh, what a trick!

The owls are hooting, in tuxedos of night,
Throwing a party, what a curious sight!
Fireflies boogie, in their glowing attire,
While crickets strum tunes that seem to inspire.

Branches shake hands, in a waltz quite absurd,
Breezes are giggling, and laughter is heard.
The moon takes a bow, in a grand old way,
As stars drop the beat, for a night full of play.

So sway and indulge in the dance of the dusk,
Among swaying silhouettes, it's all quite a husk!
With laughter and joy in the night sky's embrace,
Join in the fun, in this whimsical space.

Treetop Escapades and Earthly Whispers

A daring young chipmunk, with pockets so grand,
Scaling up trunks like a well-versed stand.
With acorns for treasure, he's brimming with glee,
Whispering secrets to leaves of the tree.

A droopy-eyed cat, perched high on a bough,
Claims she's the queen, giving us all a how.
While talking to clouds, oh what a delight,
She dreams without bounds in the soft morning light.

The branches converse, with a rustle and shake,
Plotting adventures for fun's joyful sake.
From nests to wide skies, they craft and they play,
Treetops alive with the antics of day.

So join in the whispers, the laughter, and cheer!
In the heart of the treetops, let's shed every fear.
For up in the leaves, where dreams take their flight,
Adventure awaits in the day and the night.

A Tapestry of Green Dreams

In patches of grass where the giggles run free,
Dandelions whisper, "Just pretend to be!"
With coats made of sunbeams, they laugh and they shine,
Spinning tales of mischief, oh, what a sign!

A tapestry woven with threads of pure fun,
As hedges host parties, and bushes can run.
The daisies, like jesters, put on a grand show,
As butterflies flutter, stealing the glow.

A cricket recites poems, under the stars,
While jiving tall grasses embrace all the cars.
Each leaf tells a story of laughter and cheer,
Creating a quilt of the joys we hold dear.

So come take a journey through laughter's bright seams,
In a tapestry woven of whimsical dreams.
Nature's our canvas, with colors so bold,
In the laughter of green, let our hearts unfold.

Chaotic Gardens of the Pines

In gardens where the pine trees sway,
The squirrels hold a dance today.
With acorns flying here and there,
The chaos blooms beyond compare.

A hedgehog winks beneath a bush,
As rabbits hop in a frantic rush.
The flowers giggle, petals bright,
While critters join the wild delight.

A raccoon juggles shiny stones,
While singing with a voice like drones.
The bees play tag from bloom to bloom,
Spreading laughter, filling the room.

Oh, gardens filled with playful glee,
Nature's jesters, wild and free.
With every rustle, squeak, and squeal,
The antics of the pines reveal.

The Wild Waltz of the Woodland

In woods where shadows twist and twirl,
The creatures join in a joyful swirl.
A fox in boots, a hat askew,
Leads the dance, and they follow too.

The owls hoot in rhythmic cheer,
While dancing leaves draw near and near.
A bear plays drums on fallen logs,
As dance partners—squirrels and frogs.

The wind blows soft a breezy tune,
While underfoot the flowers croon.
A raccoon moonwalks, quite a sight,
As darkness falls, the stars invite.

So waltz and jig in leafy space,
For nature knows the best of grace.
With laughter echoing through the night,
Join the woodland revelry—what a sight!

Whimsy in the Wilderness

In the cradle of the trees so tall,
A chipmunk counts his marble haul.
His tiny friends all gasp and cheer,
For every trinket brings them near.

The mushrooms wear their polka dots,
While ants parade with tiny pots.
They brew a potion, odd but bright,
Wishing on the stars tonight.

A parrot tells a joke so lame,
The rabbits laugh, they know the game.
With every twig, a giggle grows,
As nature shares its little shows.

In wilderness where whimsy thrives,
Creatures dance, and laughter drives.
Their comedy of life unfolds,
As playfulness in green enfolds.

A Symphony of Swaying Sprouts

A symphony of green takes flight,
As sprouts begin their concert bright.
They sway to rhythms of the breeze,
With leafy arms and giggling leaves.

The daisies play on tiny flutes,
While spinach sings in silly suits.
Carrots beat on wooden pails,
As laughter echoes through the trails.

A beetroot leads a jazzy beat,
With vines and roots making it sweet.
Tomatoes dance in twirling gowns,
While laughter lifts them off the ground.

A melody of blooms and stems,
Creating joy from nature's gems.
In gardens lush where smiles abound,
The symphony brings laughter round.

When Leaves Speak in Silence

A whisper floats upon the breeze,
As leaves gossip among the trees.
They chuckle softly, then take flight,
In pirouettes that end with fright.

They tumble down in playful haste,
Creating chaos, a leaf-strewn waste.
"Watch your step!" they seem to call,
As wobbly joggers start to fall.

The colors clash, a silly sight,
Red, orange, and yellow dance in light.
They swap their hues, a playful jest,
"We're nature's clowns, we're at our best!"

So when the chill begins to bite,
Remember leaves in their silly flight.
They share their secrets, soft and brief,
In rustling laughter, nature's relief.

The Crescendo of Crumbling Colors

Colors burst in a grand parade,
As leaves embark on the wacky charade.
They twirl through air like dizzy sprites,
Their bold descent ignites delights.

"Look at me!" yells a fiery red,
With yellow and brown, they spin ahead.
They form a band with giggles loud,
As squirrels hop and join the crowd.

The drum of boots on crunchy floor,
Marks the rhythm of nature's lore.
Each step a note, a joyful sound,
In the symphony of crunching ground.

Leaves take a bow, they know it's done,
A curtain call for nature's fun.
As twilight falls, they sigh and sleep,
Preparing for the secrets they keep.

Evergreen Echoes of Yesteryear

Whispers of pines, they sway and creak,
Holding tales from lips that speak.
"Once I wore a jacket green,
But now I wear this golden sheen."

They chuckle at their change of hue,
As needles drop, they bid adieu.
"Old growth, new laughs," they softly sing,
While acorns roll and chipmunks spring.

Their voices rise in playful glee,
Remembering how they used to be.
"Why stay the same?" they seem to say,
"Change is the game, come what may."

In every gust, an echo rings,
Of youthful days and silly flings.
A timeless jest, a joyous cheer,
These evergreens hold history dear.

Messy Marvels of Nature's Brush

With a splatter here and a smear right there,
Nature paints with wild, carefree flair.
Leaves are tossed like confetti bright,
Creating chaos—oh, what a sight!

Golden blobs on a navy sky,
As red and brown in heaps do lie.
"What a mess!" the trees declare,
Yet squirrels leap without a care.

The ground, a tapestry of cheer,
Piled high with laughter throughout the year.
They dive and tumble, make a show,
In this mosaic of colors aglow.

As autumn reigns with splendid grace,
Each leaf a jester in its place.
They flip and flutter, giggles abound,
In the charming ruckus they've found.

Lush Layers of Love and Loss

Under the trees, they laughed with glee,
A squirrel stole her sandwich, can't you see?
The flowers danced, in bright array,
While petals whispered things they'd say.

It's a jungle gym, but oh so sweet,
Bumbling bees, on tiny feet.
They tripped on roots, so tangled and bold,
In this leafy love, stories unfold.

Leaves falling down like confetti bright,
Turning every wrong into a light.
Yet here we are, with nature's jest,
Finding fun in every leaf-quest.

Love and loss in every hue,
As tadpoles croon tunes that feel quite new.
In this woodland, laughter rings,
Among the vines, our joy takes wing.

The Sound of Shivering Leaves

The leaves are shivering, what a sight,
Dancing to the wind's delight.
A whisper here, a giggle there,
Nature's secrets fill the air.

Crispy cracks of hidden jokes,
As branches tease the wayward folks.
A rustle here, an echo there,
Pretending to be caught unaware.

Giddy greens with laughter bright,
Waving at the startled fright.
Each gust a tickle, every swirl,
Turns serious steps into a whirl.

Under the sky, we twirl with glee,
Joining in with the rustling spree.
They flutter, they tumble, just like us,
In leafy antics, there's no fuss.

Growing Wild: Nature's Artistry

A patch of daisies in a tangle bold,
Whispers of stories, waiting to be told.
With colors wild, they laugh and play,
In nature's gallery, bright as day.

Fronds unfurl like silly grins,
While dandelions drift like whims.
A kaleidoscope, a jolly theme,
Eavesdropping on the gardener's dream.

Weeds wear crowns of unexpected grace,
As petals dance in this wild embrace.
Ribbons of sunshine, splashes of cheer,
A canvas of chaos drawing us near.

Nature's artist, with every sway,
Paints humor in a verdant display.
So when you stroll, don't miss the jest,
In each wild patch, enjoy the fest.

Secrets in the Subtle Sway

In the gentle sway, a raucous song,
Trees chuckle softly, where we belong.
Rustling secrets beneath the boughs,
Nature giggles — let's take a bow.

Branches wave like old friends near,
Weaving tales that tickle the ear.
Shadows dance, teasing the ground,
In this playful world, joy is found.

Mossy carpets, a ticklish treat,
As critters tumble on unsteady feet.
Every sway tells a story or two,
In this green delight, we're all anew.

So come and listen, and have some fun,
In the whisper of leaves, we're never done.
Join the laughter, the secrets unfold,
In nature's embrace, let the mysteries hold.

Leafy Lullabies at Twilight

Whispers of leaves in a gentle breeze,
Giggling branches sway, feeling at ease.
Crickets join in, a chirpy choir,
Twilight's tune, a leafy empire.

Dancing shadows play tag on the ground,
Beneath the boughs, laughter abounds.
A squirrel mocks with a cheeky tease,
As twilight settles, nature's keys.

The gentle rustle sings us to sleep,
While secretive critters their watch shall keep.
In pockets of dusk, humors entwine,
A lullaby leaves, soft and benign.

Chuckles and sighs from the woodland throng,
In twilight's embrace, we all belong.
Cuddling up in a leafy embrace,
In the humor of night, we find our place.

The Carnival of Changing Colors

Red, yellow, orange, a vibrant show,
Leaves lose their minds in a dizzy glow.
Like a circus, they twirl in delight,
As autumn's palette steals the night.

Crimson clowns make a leap from a tree,
While golden acrobats sway merrily.
Nature's jesters flutter and flip,
In this carnival, all take a dip.

Cotton candy clouds float in between,
Sipping on sunshine with a gleeful gleam.
Every branch shares a chuckling cheer,
As the season dons its garish gear.

When leaves wear smiles in a wild parade,
And every rustle stirs laughter unmade.
Amidst all the chaos, there's joy to be found,
In the colors that dance all around.

Nature's Unscripted Performance

A grounded stage set with leafy delight,
Where squirrels rehearse for their main flight.
Actors of green in a whimsical plot,
Nature's performance, a show that's hot.

Rabbits hop on, making their cue,
While raccoons peek from behind a view.
With butterflies casting the spotlight bright,
Improv in bloom, oh, what a sight!

A tree trunk thespian takes center stage,
Bending in laughter, a humorous age.
With gusts of wind stirring up the plot,
Every moment fresh in this lively lot.

The curtain of dusk gently falls down,
Leaving behind a twilight crown.
In the chaos of leaves, laughter rings true,
Nature's theater, starring me and you.

Harmony of Haphazard Growth

In a garden where mischief takes root,
Plants sprout askew, what a look to boot!
Dandelions giggle in their bright yellow dress,
While weeds throw parties, oh what a mess!

A sunflower leans in for a chat,
"Why can't you bloom, you silly old brat?"
The carrots beneath, they wriggle for glee,
In rows so crooked, they giggle with me.

They've mastered the art of pushing their luck,
While peeking through dirt, they find more muck.
With every sprout, the laughter takes flight,
In this haphazard growth, laughter feels right.

We'll sing and we'll dance with the herbs in the plot,
As their stories of folly become quite the trot.
For in every twist, every wild little sprout,
There's humor aplenty, without a doubt.

Nature's Jest: A Tumble of Colors

A red leaf slipped on a slick green floor,
It tumbled and rolled, what a lively score!
Golds and browns joined in a wild parade,
Chasing each other, their reason betrayed.

A blue jay giggled at the swirling show,
While squirrels debated the best way to go.
A pop of orange caused an awkward pause,
As nature erupted with laughter and applause.

Underneath branches, shadows performed,
A chaotically natural dance was formed.
Blustering breezes brought giggles galore,
As colors collided on the forest floor.

When evening fell, and the sun bid its light,
Leaves whispered secrets while twinkling bright.
The forest was grinning, a riot untamed,
In this merry spectacle, nothing was named.

Conspiracy of the Rustling Greens

Whispers of leaves stirred in the air,
A plot, they conspired, without a care.
"Let's trick the sun!" said the cheekiest sprout,
"Pretend we're flowers, let's give them a shout!"

They donned bright hues and stuck out their stems,
With sways and flutters, they foiled their own gems.
"Who needs sweet blooms when chaos delights?"
The chorus of greens sang under moonlight nights.

A squirrel chimed in, "I'll join in the fun!"
Dancing on branches, he leaped and then spun.
The wise old oak winked with a crafty grin,
As nature's own pranksters let mischief begin.

So if you wander where the greens conspire,
Listen closely, you might catch the choir.
For nature's a jester, and laughter it sows,
In secret conspiracies that nobody knows.

Whispers of the Winding Vines

Vines twisted and turned, a playful embrace,
Each curl held a secret, a comical trace.
"Let's tangle the flowers!" the red one exclaimed,
"Let's see them get out, it'll be unashamed!"

A sunflower laughed, "You think you're so sly?
Try keeping us trapped as we reach for the sky!"
So the vines played tug-of-war with each petal,
While bees buzzing loudly became quite the medal.

"Watch this!" cried the ivy, as it hopped on a fence,
"I'm the jungle gym, it makes perfect sense!"
Yet winds crept around with a teasing gust,
Sending tendrils off, which in laughter they trust.

The garden erupted in jests and in joy,
Nature's own theater, an organic ploy.
So next time you see plants, take a fine glance,
For whispers of joy are a leaf's perfect dance.

Leaves in Chaotic Dance

A fluttering leaf joined the waltz of the breeze,
Twisting and turning with utmost of ease.
Grass blades giggled beneath as they swayed,
In a festival of fun, where chaos delayed.

Spinning in circles, a whole clump of greens,
Lost in their antics, not caring for scenes.
What's this? A tumble? Oh dear! What a sight,
As a leaf did a cartwheel, to everyone's delight!

Acorns cheered loudly, "Give us some room!"
As this frenzied parade filled the autumn's gloom.
Colors jostled and jived, what a brilliant feast,
In this whimsical ball, nature filled with least.

So remember, dear friend, if you wander by,
Join the leaves in their dance, let your worries fly.
For in nature's own revel, there's always a chance,
To find laughter and joy in the leaves' mad romance.

Growth's Playful Masquerade

In the garden of jest, where leaves wear a grin,
The twigs shimmy in time, let the games begin.
Petals tickle the breeze, making laughter take flight,
A sunflower prances, oh, what a sight!

Bumblebees gossip, in their buzzing parade,
They gossip with daisies, each rumor is made.
Purple pansies wink, in their playful attire,
While ivy tells secrets, of mischief and fire.

Down where the roots twist, in whimsical dance,
Saplings are sneaking, they're up to their chance.
A ladybug giggles, on a leaf dressed in dew,
Oh, who knew that green could be so askew?

With glee in the air, nature chuckles away,
With every new sprout, there's new games to play.
Let's join in the laughter, let our spirits ignite,
As we leap through this laughter, oh, what a delight!

Truths Twisting in Tendrils

In the weave of the vines, secrets reel and unwind,
Whispers and giggles, two truths intertwined.
A chubby old snail, with wisdom profound,
Stumbles on stories, where the mischief is found.

Lush leaves play tag, in the sunlight they bask,
Fluttering ducks ask, was that all a mask?
There's humor in roots, tangled and free,
Tales of the garden, as wild as can be.

With every twist, tales bend and collapse,
Branches debate, while the shadows elapse.
The boughs become jesters, in nature's grand play,
As laughter spills forth, come join in the fray!

Under mystery's cloak, the wild truths conflate,
With each playful glance, they twirl and they skate.
Nature's own jesters, with tricks up their sleeves,
In the orchestra of green, oh, how it weaves!

The Hidden Landscape of Unkept Trails

Where paths often wander, in a tangle of green,
Nature's mischief hides in the places unseen.
Grasses play hopscotch, with dandelion heads,
While toadstools throw parties, in their sloppy threads.

A curious raccoon, with a mask of pure glee,
Keeps finding lost treasures, under each leafy tree.
The unwrought trails giggle, they dance round the bends,
Beneath the thick cover, where nonsense transcends.

Gnarled roots propose, a game of charades,
While the autumn leaves chuckle, in vibrant cascades.
A squirrel with acorns, is queen of the fun,
As shadows stretch forth, in the glow of the sun.

So wander and wander, through whimsy's embrace,
In the secrets of trails, there's joy to unlace.
From tattered old maps, new laughter will bloom,
In the wild, unkept lands, let joy find its room!

Seasonal Revelries Underfoot

Through the cracks in the pavement, blooms burst in delight,
A cheerful confetti, in colors so bright.
Tulips in tutus, dance under the sun,
While daisies in dresses, get ready for fun.

Autumn leaves tumble, in a whimsical waltz,
Each crunch underfoot is a call to joy's pulse.
Pumpkins wear smiles, on porches they gleam,
They gather round laughter, a glorious team.

Snowflakes tease noses, with their chilly approach,
While snowmen tell stories, in their frosty broach.
Sleds zoom down hills, with laughter on tow,
Each giggle and squeal, sets the spirits aglow.

In springtime, the blooms form a carnival spree,
While summer brings sunshine, all brave hearts agree.
So cherish the seasons, from winter to fall,
In nature's sure revels, there's fun for us all!

Revelry in the Rustling Thicket

In a thicket dense and bright,
Leaves giggle, a silly sight.
Branches sway with playful flair,
Nature's jesters dance in air.

Squirrels wear hats made of green,
A parade that can't be seen.
Roots tickle bugs, having fun,
Underneath the bright warm sun.

Twigs pull pranks on wayward bees,
Whispering secrets with the breeze.
Laughter echoes, oh what cheer,
As playful critters gather near.

With each rustle and each sway,
Joyful chaos leads the way.
The thicket hums a joyful tune,
A raucous dance beneath the moon.

Folly of the Flamboyant Fronds

Fronds in colors bright and bold,
Tell stories that must be told.
Prancing here with silly poses,
Twirling like they're scented roses.

Lizards laugh in leafy hats,
While frogs play leap with rusty bats.
A cockatoo on a swing so high,
Count the leaves as they pass by.

Boughs sport ribbons in the wind,
Frantically twist, each twist a grin.
Nature's jesters in the sun,
In this world, they have such fun.

Wind whistles tunes in leafy dance,
Playful hearts take every chance.
Every rustle, every sound,
Revel in joy that knows no bound.

A Tapestry of Nature's Chuckle

Amidst the greens where whispers thrive,
Leaves tell jokes that come alive.
The sun winks down with a glint,
As nature paints with every hint.

Mushrooms gather for a feast,
Silly caps on little beasts.
With giggles shared from root to tip,
Every moment, a hearty quip.

The breeze, a prankster on its lane,
Tickles trees like a sweet refrain.
Nature's palette, bright and spry,
Stitching laughter as it flies.

With every rustle, spirits soar,
A merry dance forevermore.
In this green-crafted reverie,
Nature's chuckle sets us free.

The Leafy Tricksters' Ball

In every corner, laughter bursts,
Leaves don masks for playful thirsts.
Fern fronds twist in strange designs,
As silly shadows mark their lines.

A raccoon juggles acorns well,
While owls hoot a playful spell.
Dance the tango, skip the hop,
As twinkling stars above don't stop.

The mossy ground becomes a stage,
Where critters perform, uncage their rage.
A party under the moonlight's grace,
Where every leaf finds its place.

So come along, join in the fun,
As nature laughs, til day is done.
In this leafy ball, hearts unite,
A night of jest, pure delight.

Fluttering Fronds in the Breeze

Leaves dance a jig, what a sight,
Bouncing and twirling, oh, what a flight.
Swaying and swirling, they steal the show,
Making the wind giggle, like a breeze's blow.

They whisper and chuckle, secrets they keep,
Gossiping softly while we're fast asleep.
A prank on the branches, they tease with flair,
Who knew that green could be so debonair?

In playful pursuit, they tickle the air,
Sparks of laughter in sunny glare.
A carnival swirling in shades of green,
Where sunshine's the jester, and joy is seen.

Jumping from tree to leafy delight,
Bold acrobatics take to flight.
Frolicking fronds in a whimsical tease,
With chuckles of joy riding soft summer breeze.

Enigmas of the Emerald Glade

In the woods, mystery threads tightly weave,
Underbrush giggles, you won't believe.
Nature's own puzzles, with patterns galore,
Each twist of a vine opens up a door.

Silly mushrooms wear hats for a show,
Dandelions are popping, putting on a glow.
Crickets compose melodies in tune,
With each rustle and chirp, laughter's attuned.

A raccoon's giggles echo at night,
With bushes their stage, a comedic delight.
Where pixies might tumble, just for a laugh,
In shadows of trees, they dance on a path.

Every branch holds a secret that's wild,
In these emerald enclaves, we're playful and mild.
For nature's a comedian, whirling in jest,
In the glade's rolling laughter, we find all the best.

Gnarled Branches and Daydreams

Twisted limbs reach for the vast blue,
Gnarled like the thoughts that once flew.
In shadows and sighs, they lean to impart,
Fables of whimsy, oh where do we start?

A wise old tree with a beard so long,
Sings lullabies sweetly, nature's own song.
Its bark crinkles deep with secrets to share,
While squirrels throw acorns without a care.

Branches extend in a wobbly way,
Setting the stage for a playful ballet.
In every odd twist lies a chuckle, a smile,
As nature spins tales full of wit and style.

In the depths of the forest, daydreams cavort,
With gnarled old branches hosting the sport.
Unraveling giggles in a greenery spree,
Where absurdity thrives, wild and free.

The Colorful Crowns of Trees

Treetops adorned like kings in the sun,
With hats of bright colors, oh what fun!
Flamboyant leaves flutter, a royal decree,
That nature's a courtier with glee, can't you see?

Oranges and yellows in celebrant hue,
While reds and greens join in too.
Each branch a party, twirling around,
In a carousel dance, laughter unbound.

Swaying in rhythm, the crowns take a bow,
To breezes that chuckle, we celebrate now.
For every leaf spirals, a joyous jest,
In crowns of color, our spirits invest.

Nature's confetti cascades from the trees,
With giggles and whispers that float on the breeze.
So lift up your gaze, and join in the cheer,
For the playground of foliage is vibrant and near.

www.ingramcontent.com/pod-product-compliance
Lightning Source LLC
Chambersburg PA
CBHW071833160426
43209CB00003B/284